chigger ridge

Also by Nicole Callihan:

Superloop
This Strange Garment

chigger ridge

Nicole Callihan

SELECTED BY 2023 JUDGE SANDRA LIM
SERIES EDITOR JENNIFER BARBER

THE WORD WORKS
Washington, D. C.

THE WORD WORKS

P.O. Box 42164
Washington, D.C. 20015
editor@wordworksbooks.org
Author photograph: Erin Silber
Cover art: *Taking It All In*, Kelly Edwards
Cover design: Susan Pearce

ISBN: 978-1-944585-82-2

Acknowledgments

I'm grateful to the editors of the following journals where some of these poems first appeared:

Scalawag Magazine: "clothes" & "music"

STILL: The Journal: "smoke," "pellet," "weeds," & "where"

The Waywiser Press: "chigger ridge" & "day," finalist entry for the Anthony Hecht Poetry Prize

Contents

There was earth inside them, and / they dug.

—Paul Celan, tr. John Felstiner

chigger ridge

there the sun
did not rise
until we'd been
up for hours
then it
crowbarred
the day
turned the trees
from lead
to silver
turned the dead
to face
the river
the night again
the poet
told me to
go to sleep
wait until
i dreamed
of an angel
and when
the angel speaks
the poet said
listen to her
notice the color
of her dress
blue jean blue

then wake up
and write it
down in
the valley
all night i slept
i was naked
but i was not cold
and lo
i say unto you
the angel
did her bidding
and lo
she offered me
a slopjar
and lo a cat's eye
marble
and lo she told me
to be not afraid
of the soul
and the grass
on the ledge
in which i lay
made me itch
with a violence
i'd carry away
if the portrait
of the self
is a pallet
on the floor
if the floor
is as hard as

the night outside
if the night's
got nothing
on the old man
out back
you say self
and point
to my chest
but what of these
trees this still
star-soaked sky
what of the
cuts and tongues
and tins of meat
can be cleaved
from the girl
on the ridge
who in the dark
with a cleaver
stands and lo
i say unto you
lo i say come
with me lo

and what we dug deep into dug into us too

mine

other mountains had iron or coal
something good beneath us we had
nothing we panned for fool's gold
and though it shined it was not real
and the men who owned what lay beneath
our earth pillaged us for many moons
but finding absence moved deeper uphill
in west virginia they strip her still
layer after layer dust to dust
sometimes it's better to be hollow
to have nothing is to have nothing to take

moon

ain't nothing was right in those hills
dogs humped cats and cousins cousins
like took to unlike and made it like
all winter the loblollies violated the moon
so you couldn't see for shit
couldn't feel to feel couldn't even try
and trying didn't mean nothing more
than digging up a can of tuna from the cupboard
if you strained your ears you might hear crying
but probably you'd just hear what you have
ass elbows what the doctors call murmur

night

the wolf came but the wind howled louder
what is known is known is not known
in the hills the children's teeth rot out
girls hung out to dry get left to die
bad water bad blood bad boy
documents to sign blackbarnian warblers
bills gone unpaid listen wolves kill the sickly first
which is to say pretend you're pretty
and spin in that terrible wind

pellet

among the things we shot off the barbed wire fence
an old plastic doll head a couple of tins of peas
about a hundred sundrop bottles their labels
melted off by storm and toil with one hand
malachi pointed the gun to the sky the other
he put down my pants i sucked on his earlobes
and fingers like this i asked he steadied
my arm you gotta keep your eye above the target
staring straight will choke you we'd shoot and pet
swat skeeters until dusk when nobody called us home
i love you i said into the air you wouldn't know
love if it bit you in the ass

where

out past boone start taking rights
right at the crook right at the hairpin
right by the old dead dog bend
right when you see the cross right when
the flowers bloom when they stop
blooming right when your heart becomes
something other to the left of your soul
right when you get brave enough to say
soul right when you stop right here
right sided right minded right winged
right footed right dreamed right there

day

to imagine there had been dusty apples would mean
apples would mean there had been apples once maybe in jars
in some cellar jarred up like down at the schoolhouse
baby girl in a jar fetus the science teacher scolded fetus
but he was the kind who believed in monkeys feed us
this day our daily mush let us not be hungry
let our bodies not invisible be let there be a tree
where something grows let us not be mere specimens
when all things commence let us among the things be

class

the external gills typical of amphibians
exposed to the environment if you gargle
enough frog eggs you might learn
how to breathe if you borrow enough cash
you might be able to put enough gas in the tank
to get you to town o stagnant water frog embryo
stink of your stink somewhere there's a machine
that can look inside and tell you why it hurts

scrub your dark places with a washrag

clothes

the fog which stitches us in seams us makes us seem
unseemly clasping clasps sewing me into this old blue dress
my love is knot is all tied up o safely pinned body unravel
unwind hot southern pick me up and deliver me
with flowers from evil to grace blind girl blind cat
can't see your hand in front of your face i keep thinking
somebody will save me but it's hard enough to make it
to the store around here let alone cut coupons
let alone find redemption or a shirt that buttons and is stainless

hole

maybe deepsummer you'd make your way down
to the swimming hole but mostly you just dragged
the old tin tub to the pump let the water warm
in the sun if you were lucky a little lye a washrag
if cleanliness is next to godliness if godliness
is next to the flowers if the flowers your fingers
your pits if the pit of a prune gets spit in your hand
if the water never warms the body stays dirty

inside

you can't blame the land for what dwells inside
or what does not bother to dwell
cause you ain't got Jesus nor man nor love
the sickness rises to offer you company
LOVE's too many hairpins away
the darkness inside still blooms darkness
sprouts hair and teeth and baby fingernails
and at first you feel better you feel goooood
cause you finally got something something at all
walking in the hills the sickness sings you hymns
in bed at night it makes you utter your prayers
so when it sours you can't hate its stink
cause it comes from your very you your only you
your ugly little you you you

remedy

she's got answers to questions you didn't know you had
how to have a baby how to get rid of a baby what to do
if you get cauliflowers on your privates sassafrass
spearmint lard snakeroot cut grass kerosene ginger
for worms it's two parts brown sugar one part turpentine
sister bunny pie-maker and healer if body is to body as soul
to lump in your throat to belly thigh lump titty lump
lump of clay of grace everybody knows not to sweep
under the bed of the sick but here's something else
let the birds use your hair for their nest and you'll go crazy
if this happens tie a string around a crabapple tree
there in its shade bury your dreams

smoke

the old man's knee was a horse and the horse
was named smoke and the old man's sweater
was made of smoke and his fingers and his face
and if you breathe just right you're smoke too
the horses got so hungry they started eating
the trees but the trees had no more fruit
than the bowls that were earthen empty
and blue a sky tipped up on its hind legs
bucking and mad mustang moon back room
if you dig deep enough into the ashtray
you might find something worth smoking

dead

of the deceased of the pennies on his eyes
got from the shack that sells penny candy
old bread ranch doritos newport blues
of the daisies the girls carry from his house
this is the body which delimits the soul
this is the soul derailed deranged devoid
of the softness of the snow that fell
that falls is falling for the deceased
the preacher has good words tells how
before the dead was dead he was a man
before a man a boy who fished on a rock
deployed deplaned deflated detached
catfish breath dry eyes hunt for dark clothes

sleep

perchance to dream perchance the ocean
or hollywood or new york city perchance
two shiny quarters and a cheerwine machine
perchance sky perchance the soft skin
behind malachi's ear perchance the old man
gets his hands cut off perchance walking
along the river walking and walking and
perchance you come across a wolf pup or
a dead body perchance you lay next to it
for a long while cry into its cold shoulder
carry it home and hide it under the house

lord

i the undersigned have been more evil than i
would like to admit in these papers these papers
themselves are dressed in the devil's clothes and i
in the devil's wife's sweater and in the pants of the devil's
wife's best friend who seeing that i had bled myself
in church one sunday showered me with maxipads
elastic bands panties bigger than all the hills
o jesus i don't know how much smaller and weaker
you could have made me can't tell love from pity
but if to inherit the earth is this i do not want the earth

down in my heart

places

we couldn't even get to town let alone
out of town foot down hair down
no place would've had us anyway
slop for a mouth potbelly soggy eyed
australia bethlehem china d.c. egypt
florida gastonia heaven and if not heaven well
we didn't have purgatory it was hell
or wings one spring malachi's uncle caught fire
in the toy section of walmart making meth
with a child's chemistry set got sent away
but he came back wasn't any different
if anything he was just more the same

dream

for days i soured on dreams on the fifth
i wrapped the filth around me and made peace
with what was left of myself in the dream
walked one thousand miles to knock on my own door
and got no answer when i tried the knob
i let myself in once did nothing more than fall
asleep on the pallet on which i was already sleeping
what happens when the body we discover is our own
after the sixth night i rose and listened to the back room
where the old man slept light would come i told myself
and so i swept the corners good and hard

seed

on the porch the old man takes his knife
to the apple you ever seen the flesh
inside holds the flat of the apple high
a rattler snakes by i might pick this scab
til the end of days might make it bleed
til the sea parts til the loneliest seed
can't find shape enough or rain
if the porch of the body becomes the porch
of the mind if memory sits in the rocker
and makes up lies if in the crawl space
the yellow cat with its broken spine dies
well then what's to come of the star inside

eels

let us go then you and i let us let go let us
be the eye pry the eye pie-eyed if this be
world enough and time if this be the world we
were granted would take for granted would we
all afternoon i spied eels in the stream spied me

crimes

case of the one-eyed snake case of the pickled heart
case of the willies of the blues case of the beast drunk down
of the girl against the old man against the girl against the girl

weeds

kudzu kills everything but itself
crawls up into the space of the green
up your thighs into your throat
out back a billy goat on a rope
jug of milk small shame wild forsythia
pushes through i wonder the river
pounds the rocks pound the sky
pounds the hot nickel sun pounds
the old man's hands pound me
come august i swim anyway
if only through the thick wild weeds

house

not that the house still stands but that it ever stood
not that the tree that rots rots but that it ever bloomed
we were an accidental people our accidental hands
built accidental houses with accidental wood
i liked to sit and watch the old man sweat and hope he'd fall
down river downstream down home down
dilly down the only way to remember the west is to remember
where you last spotted the sun smoke rises from the chimney
from the mill and from that which smolders
for that which is nearly dead still burns hot and deep

frost

the old man says the spring i was a glimmer
the ground shimmered cold and somebody
found some good bones to simmer and everybody
sipped and supped and it seemed like things would be ok
would be a little wax-wrapped pie in an old leather bag
but the wind howled hard and the shimmer turned frost
wouldn't have been much to pick the green tomatoes
from the vine and let them ripen in a cardboard box
in the front room but nobody did the tomatoes died
and though bitter as gall the old man
dug his thumbs in and ate them anyway

gutter

guttural glut guts glory what you might string
along the roof to dry out and or proclaim victory
victory itself the victor vigor valor vim vinegar
vanity vanity on which you might place a hairbrush
backside backslide slid back into a shadow
that which is evidence of a body as made by sunlight
or other light source but what evidence is there of more
in the field the girl holds her empty hands to the sky
is she praying probably not then what then what

lo

glad

but everything wasn't always terrible i'd save
my dimes in stacks of ten to buy math workbooks
and sometimes the sky got so blue i could
feel my heart pounding in my throat to walk
along a river even if you have never walked
along another river is to know other rivers
to find a longing for something
is to long to press that shapelessness
into your palm under your tongue is to begin
to understand its contours in the snow
playing dead is to feel the fast flicker of being

psalm

to stand on the mountain and try to find words
for things to try to find the order of the things
to try to find the letters that make the words
that turn utterance into something he or she or they
might toad firefly longing understand to incant
enchant enchanted be the meek for they shall inherit
the tongues of their ancestors to change your fate
sit by the stream and think of an animal
you'd like to bury yourself in now hold that feeling
to a flame now spitwash your dark now become other

sermons

and lo the bruised reed shall be balm to the soul
and lo thy eye is blind and thy ear deaf
and lo thou shall not sow seed on rocky ground
and lo the vanity of your tears shall drown you
and lo the weight of glory shall cripple you

flight

must've been spring everything was shining
with meltedness and i met malachi by the river
first it seemed he was just splitting a chicken
and the looking itself gnawed at my hunger
but he'd strung the feathers on clothesline
there on the ground in a sawed-off sundrop bottle
a robin's eggs blood and feathers from all sorts
of birds figuring out how to fly malachi said
you should be ashamed of yourself i told him
then i let him kiss my neck a little then we sat
in shame together and smoked beneath the sky

interrupt

rupture rapture a knock on the door ain't
nothing but wind back to sleep babyface
back to the pallet belly to the pallet back
to the creek groan of the floor back
home forget back home back here but
back home you got a lock of hair you call hers
but it's yours really and not even a lock
but mess pulled from a brush
even if it was a lock it wouldn't have a soul

escape

if self is to self as self is to other then
the crawlspace in which the self
has hunkered is the crawlspace
in which the self will stay cat stench
and rain and moldy wrapping paper
must've been a time somebody thought
to make something pretty if the words
in the book are the sole salvation
if the sole salvation is the only salve
then may your young self be eclipsed
may you become what you never were

ajar

cold metal knob i might forever feel
beneath my fingertips the old man
had won a horse from someone the snow
was thighdeep skinny old mare tied
to a tree and me in the kitchen looking
past the dirty curtains pane of glass
paned glass pang to stir the fire might
keep it alive might keep you let down
your hair girlwoman find peace in the pines

monkey

carnival must've left it malachi found it
behind the walmart in town brought it
to me for valentines seems crazy now
but then it was just a monkey
what's a girl to do with a monkey
what's a girl to do what's a girl
what's a matter what's a matter babyface
why so blue listen if you can make a monkey
dance you will never go hungry

finch

the hand is as empty as summer
as a closet as the space between the we
between the old man's knees the old man's
teeth old man's dirty fingers and then
the rain always after days passeth the rain
girl you can sit in the bush and pray all day
hold your hands to the sky but empty breeds
empty nothing gives way to the same

lace

drawers lined with velvet roses i crawl into
the church lady's secrets i a spider a thief
a babysitter a whore and her with her own
privacies her privates her pretty pretty pretties
the space between the self and other becomes
see-through a window a fishing net a fish
flung from the sea careless as me i rub
the fabric on my face breathe in the musk of it
the web then footsteps you dirty you dirty little
i run home breathless mud cakes my feet

hide it under a bush o no

rock

water takes granite granite takes scissors
scissors take paper paper takes words
words float downriver river takes fish
fish takes worm worm takes blood
blood takes heart takes heat take heart
girlwoman take heart old man take heart
lice lady take heart fucking government
and when you get heartsick of taking heart
take the scissors to your hair take a hat
to hide your shame let all these things settle
in the bed of the stream amen

secret

of the color the shape the exact dimensions
of the whispers the old man with his knife
to his apple on his porch in late may says
well you never seen a fish quite that size
and with eyes that bugged out like a beast
begging to be tamed only stain on me
i got from picking the prickle of blackberries
as god and wind and my daddy's dead body
be my witness your whispers are only yay big
but my truth is plain and massive as sky

music

pinpricks of light of sound of spinning angry
in the rain malachi and i never danced or didn't
know what to call it if there is no music no steps
then is it dancing in the forest body on body
breath on breath prickle of pine needles prickle
of tingles in the spine the groin little groan
little muscle a head on a shoulder by a river
a river in a body near the shoulder of the road
and the mouth of the river and the shoulder
of the other and the rhythm within pulsing
pulsing the wolf's steady heartbeat

spoon

sense is something other people might make
might try to make take me on this mountain
isn't even a mountain more like a hill
of sweetgum and ashes a wall in the kitchen
with twenty old spoons for décor
but not a soup nor a jelly nothing
to dip the rounded side in i keep thinking
i'll come to understand what i've been
put here for but then i get desirous
and forget to wonder or the old man
wanders in and says boo just to scare me
and i go on the porch and shake until it rains

keeper

summers you couldn't hardly step in the river
without a catfish knocking up against your shin
the old man on his rock taught me and malachi
which ones to throw back in and which to keep
in the big plastic bucket to haul down to the market
try to get something for them he ain't all bad
malachi said of the old man and i ain't neither
he said and you neither we were all mostly bad
it seemed but there was some small pulsing core
that doled out love or fire or would be the thing
if we were lucky that kept us

break

it ain't all bad having you around
the old man says but probably just because
i remember eggs and he can't remember
much of anything let alone get us fed
the whole house warm and quiet
you get used to what you get used to
sometimes you just have to be the self you are
break bread drown it in buttermilk
wash your supper down find something
akin to forgiveness don't worry soon enough
you'll be somebody else

glory

of morning dew of the air of the earth that
was beneath us earth inside us how we scooped it
with our fingers how our fingers smelled forever
of it and of ourselves of the spaces between
what could be named of the wall downriver
where you can find a hole to stick in what you please
of the please itself of the pleasing the pleas
o this little light o mine of the shining the light
behind the trees what seeps inside if you wait
long enough and unlearn your stubborn limbs

call

where i'm calling from is sticks and rain and afternoon
sun a sweet slick sweat on the lip of a stream
if i had another nickel i'd rub it with this one shine
it up real good this is a moon and this is a man and
this the road and this the dirt and if you spin long
enough you'll fall the self stands alone under
the sky the self walks alone sleeps alone alone
is the self the self alongside the self alongside
the dream of some self that some self once dreamed

Epilogue

Years have passed, and I have taken unlikely refuge in the academy. Occupying a small, square office, I try to keep my fingernails clean. I do not know how people become people, or, really, even what a person is. My talk is small, and I remain likely to get distracted by the light. In order to quell my long-lived hunger, I give myself strange prompts: one word title, I say; don't mention the word mother; who was the youest you you can imagine? But what does this I know about that you? Nothing? Everything? In these quarters, I am as unseen as I was on chigger ridge. Lo, the blinking cursor is the decades-old cat's eye marble knocking around in the slop jar is me.

About the Author

Nicole Callihan writes poems and stories. Her books include *This Strange Garment* (Terrapin 2023), *SuperLoop* (Sock Monkey 2014), and the poetry chapbooks *The Deeply Flawed Human*, *Downtown*, and *ELSEWHERE* (with Zoë Ryder White), as well as a novella, *The Couples*. Her work has appeared in *The Kenyon Review*, *Colorado Review*, *Conduit*, *The American Poetry Review*, and as a Poem-a-Day selection from the Academy of American Poets. She has received support from the Rockefeller Foundation, Ludwig Vogelstein, and the Sustainable Arts Foundation. *SLIP*, which won an Alma Award, will be published by Saturnalia in Spring 2025. Find out more at nicolecallihan.com.

About the Artist

Kelly Edwards is a watercolor and mixed media artist and owner of Arbor Gallery in Carmel, NY, who finds inspiration in the beauty of nature, expressionism, art nouveau and the watercolor medium itself. Becoming an artist in order to develop an ability to counter a need for control, she allows herself to embrace the unexpected in her work. Her artwork has been exhibited in LAND Gallery in Pawling, NY, Emerge Gallery in Saugerties, NY, and featured at Putnam Arts Council. See more at kellyedwardsart.com.

About The Word Works

Since its founding in 1974, The Word Works has steadily published volumes of contemporary poetry and presented public programs. Its imprints include The Washington Prize, The Tenth Gate Prize, The Hilary Tham Capital Collection, and International Editions.

Monthly, The Word Works offers free programs in its Café Muse Literary Salon. Starting in 2023, the winners of the Jacklyn Potter Young Poets Competition are presented in the June Café Muse program.

As a 501(c)3 organization, The Word Works has received awards from the National Endowment for the Arts, the National Endowment for the Humanities, the D.C. Commission on the Arts & Humanities, the Witter Bynner Foundation, Poets & Writers, The Writer's Center, Bell Atlantic, the David G. Taft Foundation, and others, including many generous private patrons.

An archive of artistic and administrative materials in the Washington Writing Archive is housed in the George Washington University Gelman Library. The Word Works is a member of the Community of Literary Magazines and Presses.

wordworksbooks.org

About the Tenth Gate Prize

The Tenth Gate Prize honors mid-career poets writing in English. Entry is open to authors of at least two previously published full-length poetry collections (excluding chapbooks, self-published volumes, and forthcoming titles). A prize of $1000 and publication of the full-length collection is awarded annually. Kasey Jueds served as Series Editor 2018-2022, and Jennifer Barber began serving as Series Editor in 2023. The winning manuscript is selected by an outside judge. The submission period is June 1 through July 15.

Leslie McGrath founded the series in 2014 to honor Jane Hirshfield's essay collection *Nine Gates: Entering the Mind of Poetry* and each winner's sustained dedication to developing a unique poetics.

Past Winners:

Jennifer Barber, *Works on Paper*, 2015
Carolyn Guinzio, *A Vertigo Book*, 2020
Christine Hamm, *Gorilla*, 2019
Lisa Lewis, *Taxonomy of the Missing*, 2017
Doug Ramspeck, *Blur*, 2021
Brad Richard, *Parasite Kingdom*, 2018
Jennifer Richter, *Dear Future*, 2022
Roger Sedarat, *Haji As Puppet*, 2016
Lisa Sewell, *Impossible Object*, 2014

Printed in the USA
CPSIA information can be obtained
at www.ICGtesting.com
CBHW050024140624
9755CB00006BA/8